BLUFF YOUR WAY IN
IN
THEATRE

FIDELIS MORGAN

RAVETTE BOOKS

Published by Ravette Books Limited
Egmont House
8 Clifford Street
London W1X 1RB
(071) 734 0221

First printed 1986
Reprinted 1989, 1992
Series Editor – Anne Tauté

Cover design – Jim Wire
Printing & Binding – Cox & Wyman Ltd.
Production – Oval Projects Ltd.

The Bluffer's Guides® is a
Registered Trademark

The Bluffer's Guides® series is based
on an original idea by Peter Wolfe.

For the make up on the cover,
grateful thanks are due to:

Charles H. Fox Ltd. Theatrical Make Up
Suppliers, Covent Garden, London W1

CONTENTS

to
Phil, Dave
and Big G

INTRODUCTION

In theatrical matters a bluffer's life is a dicey business. Whereas the average bus driver would not feel compelled to advise a brain surgeon which scalpel to use, nor would a hairdresser be driven to criticise the choice of valves made by an electrical engineer, when it comes to the theatre every Tom, Dick and Harry has his own analysis of where the writer, director and actors went wrong. On top of this there are hundreds of people who have spent 40 years or more locked in a library becoming specialists in grand guignol acting in Serbo-Croatia between 1857 and 1859.

There is absolutely no point in attempting to learn by rote a list of world dramatists from 1000 B.C. to today, together with the names of all their plays, because you are sure to recount the amazing life stories of the women playwrights of the Restoration to someone who has just written a book about them.

When surrounded by so many experts of varying degree, the only advice we can offer is the old adage: 'If you've got a hump-back put a frill round it' (i.e. make them jealous of your ignorance by passing it off as freshness and originality).

On the other hand there is no point looking an absolute fool. The theatre, like any business, is packed with jargon designed to exclude the uninitiated. You do not want to spend the best part of a discussion on the problems facing Equity wondering why actors should get so heated about what's going on in the Stock Exchange. Nor when an actor greets you with "I'm giving a salad in the park!" do you want to labour under the misapprehension that you have been invited to a picnic.

You do not need to know everything about world theatre from the Fol de Rols to Fuente Ovejuna. You simply need enough facts to get you by.

Don't forget to apply any knowledge at all to get the conversation where you want it. For example: when someone tries to impress you by saying that they're off to the Pitlochry Festival Theatre, simply tell them that Pitlochry is the birthplace of Pontius Pilate (son of one of the Romans in Britain), and you've steered them away from any discussion of plays you've never heard of.

And never forget you're not the only bluffer. In the world of Theatre *everybody* is one. Actors who talk of having "something in the pipeline" are simply out of work; directors who discuss their new "interpretation" are describing a production everyone else thought of years ago and dismissed as nonsense, and so it goes on and on.

The most important weapon you have is your own confidence in the fact that you know practically nothing, and your determination to keep it that way.

Theatre People

The actors' trade union, **Equity,** manages to get into the national news twice a year: once to announce that the entire population of Albania, Nepal, Upper Volta and Swaziland added together is less than the total number of British actors without a job, and later in the year to claim that they are fighting off more left-wing take-over bids than the Labour Party. Apart from that they don't do much.

Equity's membership is composed of actors, directors, designers, opera singers, stage-managers and both ballet and belly dancers.

The actor Michael Wilding once said that you can recognise **Actors** by the glazed look that comes into their eyes when the conversation wanders away from themselves. They also seem to talk 700 decibels louder than the average man in the street.

Directors are far more chameleon-like. Bad Directors often wear leather jackets, cuban heeled boots, and speak when they're not spoken to. They give the actor such helpful advice as "Follow the thrust of the subtext and the momentum of your given circumstances, and let the units' impetus mark the rhythm of the dynamic." And an actor in deep trouble may be comforted with the note "Your explorations are uncontained." Good Directors, a much rarer breed, can only be recognised by an intelligent twinkle in the eye.

In the world of opera and ballet, **Tenors** are fat, **Basses** are tall, **Ballerinas** are practically midgets and for the others, your guess is as good as ours.

Auditions

Each production that you see begins its working life with **auditions.** These are generally held in a theatre, usually onstage on someone else's set. So that a potential King Henry V can find himself summoning the troops to battle in the oak-beamed chintzy front room of the Vicarage at Little Muckton-Under-Ouse. The actor stands in a blast of light on the stage whilst the directors sit smugly in the stalls shouting "Thank you SO much ... Next!" Sometimes auditions are held in dusty church halls and, if you are very unlucky, in seedy West London hotel rooms.

There are two principal ways actors discover where and when a certain audition is to take place:

1. The artist's **Agent** (a person who takes between 5 and 15 per cent of the actor's wages and 100 per cent of the blame for anything that the actor is miserable about) arranges an audition on his or her client's behalf.
2. The artist hears about it on the **grapevine**, which is an unsavoury method of picking up as much information as possible from friends who failed to get the job yesterday, or who are eagerly awaiting a **recall** for tomorrow.

It is rumoured that some actors read about auditions in *The Stage*, the so-called organ of the theatrical profession. In any week one might expect to find 53 advertisements for topless waitresses in Beirut and one for the production of *Godspell* which closed last Saturday.

Some actors, of course, no longer have to audition and are merely phoned and offered the part. These are usually the actors whose name appears above the title on the poster for the show in question.

There are various job-descriptions for the work (**parts** or **roles**) available: **The Lead**, is what most people seem to play (or **give**). It is not uncommon to meet twelve actors, all with different parts in the same production, every one of whom claims to be playing the lead. Never question this or you might have to listen to a diatribe about how the play may be *called* Hamlet, but in fact it is the role of Osric that makes or breaks it.

Actors who can actually admit that they are not the lead describe their parts as:

a. a cameo
b. small, but meaningful
c. a spit and a cough
d. bread-and-butter work

These honest folk generally describe themselves as jobbing or middle-range actors. They often wear reefer jackets, paisley scarves, twill trousers and hush-puppies. Men and women alike.

A couple of smallish parts are specifically described as **the salads** — Salerio and Solanio in *The Merchant of Venice*. Hence "I'm giving a Salad in the Park" translates as "I'm playing Salerio or Solanio at the Open Air Theatre, Regent's Park."

Early in most actors' careers they will be expected to take non-speaking roles known as **walk-ons**, **extras & supers**. They might also **understudy**, or **cover** one of the leads. If they're unlucky.

Venues

All of these parts will be played in one of the following theatres:

The West End — which includes all the older style theatres in Central London, and where productions are generally funded by production companies backed by **angels**, rich fools with money to throw down the drain.

The National or **The RSC** — publicly funded labyrinthine buildings with no windows and nylon carpets which give off more static electricity than Battersea Power Station.

The Fringe — draughty basements, attics and rooms above pubs with little money, where general bonhomie and artistic ardour are supposed to compensate for the miserable lack of comfort.

A Number One Tour — a left-over from the days when there were hundreds of touring theatres which were rated on a sliding scale similar to the Michelin guide. Nowadays, whether the tour visits Edwardian theatres, civic buildings or school sports halls, no one ever admits to being less than a number one tour.

Rep — Regional, generally publicly funded, theatres. There is a strict hierarchy of reps, which is subject to sudden and unaccountable change. The acquisition of a job at Barrow-in-Furness Rep might inspire gasps of admiration on a Monday, but if you mention it the following Wednesday you will find yourself being shunned at parties and refused a table at Joe Allens.

Rehearsals

Rehearsals take about four weeks, although current fashion allows anything up to six months. Once, rehearsals were adequately described by the French word for them — répétitions. But lately, a tendency has developed to hold **organic** rehearsals, which swing between nursery-school-type game playing and dry, academic discussions of the influences of post-Freudian floccinaucinihilipilification of the play in hand.

The first rehearsal usually begins with a **read-through**, where the play is read through. In the old days this task fell to the playwright, whose standards of reading must have so appalled the members of the cast and director that they now do it themselves. The actors sit in a semi-circle and mumble and mutter their way slowly through the piece. The few actors who shout and read with much bravado on these occasions can generally be depended upon to give the worst performances in the finished production.

It is worth noting that some actors use the Read-through as a chance to weigh up the potential bedability quotient of the rest of the cast. When not speaking, these actors can be found scanning the bodies of the people they fancy and giving them points out of ten.

The director sits at one end of the rehearsal room behind a desk littered with dirty coffee cups, chewed dog-ends of (usually French) cigarettes, screwed up pieces of paper, and mangled copies of the **script**. Next to him/her sits (if the theatre is rich enough to have one) the **Assistant Director**, and the **Assistant Stage-Manager** (A.S.M.), whose job it is to write down the actor's moves as they are set, or **blocked**.

Some directors (and these are almost always actors manqués) insist on getting up every two seconds, rushing out onto the acting area, and giving the actor what is meant to be the definitive reading of a line. At these moments it takes all the self-control the actor has not to burst into derisive laughter. However, actors with a bit of experience have learnt to nod seriously, holding their chin in one hand, and say with a tone of dawning enlightenment,

"Aaaaaaaaaah I seeeeeeee!" and then continue doing exactly what they were doing before.

Actors who are not in the scene being rehearsed can generally be found in the nearest pub, where they claim to be learning their lines. Actors who are in the scene, but not in the particular bit of it that is being rehearsed, huddle around the edge of the room on uncomfortable benches and folding chairs. The least intelligent make a big show of doing *The Independent* or *Guardian* crosswords, the latter a compulsory part of an actor's uniform.

Some bring their knitting or tatting or sewing or macramé (this style of rehearsal time-filling is no longer a female prerogative). Some make a big show of modesty while chuckling over the fan-mail which arrived with the morning's mail, and which they posted to themselves the day before. Fired by the electric atmosphere of the rehearsal room, others sleep.

Towards the end of the rehearsal period actors experience the runs:

Word runs – Where the actors, without doing any of the moves, speak the play as though for radio.

Speed runs – Where the actors perform the play as though it is an L.P. being played at 45 r.p.m. Some actors are marvellous at this, others just go on doing it as they have always done it. When speed runs are taken at a real lick they are exhilarating and hilarious for all.

Dry runs – Where the actors instead of playing out (as an opera singer might 'sing out'), the whole thing is done for accuracy of words and moves and not strength of acting.

The rehearsal period comes to a ghastly climax with the technical rehearsal (**The Tec**), which is usually a stop-start rehearsal lasting all day and into the early hours of the morning after, during the course of which the designer discovers that none of the dresses fit through the doors; the lighting designer realises that his lighting plot overloads the system and causes black-outs throughout a five-mile radius of the theatre; the stage-management is finally made to understand that when the director asked for the back wall of the stable scene to be covered in yokes, he had not said yolks; the director sends the assistant director out to buy valium, and the actors, not used to being ignored, try to regain attention by making up new lines, coming on with their flies undone and their wigs on back-to-front, falling off the edge of the stage and breaking their ankles, or collapsing in the wings and being rushed to hospital where tests confirm that they are suffering from a little known condition called everyone-forgot-me-during-the-tec-syndrome.

The final or Dress Rehearsal, (**The Dress**), is a much more sombre affair. It is usually conducted exactly as a public performance would be (i.e. no stopping if anything goes wrong), and the stage manager times it with a stop-watch. This is the moment when the actors, through a miasma of fear, begin to realise what they've let themselves in for. Meanwhile, everyone else in the building, now beyond terror, starts making remarks like "worse things happen at sea", and "que sera sera!". Some even trot out the old and utterly falacious adage — "Bad dress; good show." By this time the director has mentally left the production and has started working on his or her next.

13

Performance

The First Night, a social occasion providing much the same pleasures as the rattle of the tumbrils and the swish of the guillotine, is attended by:

1. **Critics** (the Mesdames Defarge of the audience)

2. **Friends** of the cast (a raggle-taggle band of aristocrats in disguise) mumbling prayers of relief that they're not on the other side of the curtain.

3. A group of self-styled **culture vultures** determined to have as vile an evening as possible (the Mob).

As a result, the first-night audience is entirely different from any other, and the noises coming from it can be broken down as follows:

1. From the critics, a black and ominous silence. This does not necessarily indicate that they're not thoroughly enjoying themselves. It is their feeble attempt to prevent the other critics knowing what they actually think.

2. From the friends, hopelessly misguided support in the form of screams of delight at each tired joke, occasional attempts to lead the audience into unspontaneous applause after each character enters or exits, and cat-calls and wolf-whistles at the end.

3. From the culture-vultures, the eternal rustling of programmes and sweet-papers.

Afterwards there is a frantic rush backstage to congratulate the actors, however bad they've been.

The point is, you see, they got through it and didn't take a flight to Papua New Guinea during the interval.

Backstage

One can sometimes get past the **Stage-door man** with a breezy familiarity: "Hello there, Fred. Hope you're keeping well! What number's Miss X?" But the stage-door man is on the whole a very hard nut to crack. Most of them are well weathered against bluffers, even those with a £5 note hidden in the palm of their hand. The best bet for anyone with a built-in compass is to attempt the **Pass Door**, a door marked 'Private' which links the auditorium to the backstage area. But this can be lethal because, backstage, every theatre is indistinguishable from the Hampton Court Maze.

Presuming you have made your way into the inner sanctum, or **dressing room** where the offending actors sit surrounded by good-luck telegrams, greasy wigs on hat stands, and disgusting stumps of **slap** (or make-up) strewn over a counter, itself covered with a small hand-towel or doily, you then encounter a whole new language and many strange customs, which must be observed if you are not to seem the leprous outsider that you obviously are.

Firstly, take it as read you will be addressed as 'darling'. This is partly meant in affection, and partly because the actors haven't a clue who you are, even if you are their husband or wife. The adrenalin of the evening's performance and the relief that it's over are so overwhelming that your name is literally irrelevant.

As a member of the audience, you have been one of the **Punters**, or **bums on seats**. Perhaps you sat in the gallery or **Gods**, or in the back of the gallery or **Woods**. Perhaps you were lucky enough to get a free ticket or **Comp**, perhaps most of the audience did, in which case it was a **papered house**.

All play titles will be abbreviated, usually to one word; for instance, *The Merchant of Venice* becomes Merchant, *A Midsummer Night's Dream* becomes The Dream and *Look Back In Anger* becomes Anger. There are a few exceptions; *Nicolas Nickleby* is Nick-Nick, *Les Misérables* is The Glums and the adaptation of *A La Recherche du Temps Perdu* called *A Waste of Time* is The Proust.

The architectural terms which must be understood are:

Tabs — Curtains.

Wings — Offstage sides of the stage.

Pros (pronounced pross) — Proscenium arch.

Cyc (pronounced syke) — Cyclorama, or tight screen-like curtain round the back of the stage.

Flies — Area above the stage where pieces of scenery are 'flown'.

Traps — Holes in the stage through which actors can emerge as though from the bowels of the earth.

Iron — The safety curtain.

Flats — Areas of canvas, stretched on wood and painted, which make up the walls of the set.

Floats – Footlights (now rarely used except in pantomime.

Green Room – A rat-infested hole where the actors relax.

Some simple but essential elements of performance jargon are:

To dry – To forget one's words.

To fluff – To mess up one's words.

To corpse – To break into an unrehearsed fit of uncontrollable laughter.

Perf – Performance.

Props – Properties, items used on stage.

Pracs – Props which actually work, like lighters and soda syphons.

Business (i.e. 'Now let's put in a bit of business') – Over-acting with a prop, usually a soda syphon. Not to be confused with **The Business** meaning the theatrical profession.

Rounds – Spontaneous bursts of applause usually on an actor's entrance or exit.

Cue – The line after which an actor enters or has to speak his/her own line.

Doobries – Anything you've forgotten the name of.

The Curtain, or **The Call** — Line up of actors at the end of each performance.

Your **Call** — Time at which each individual actor is expected to be in the theatre or the rehearsal room, i.e. "What time is my call tomorrow?"

The Run — Length of time during which a play is performing at a theatre, not to be confused with The Runs (see page 12).

Then there are the time calls – which are all five minutes fast, since this is supposed to be the length of time it takes an actor to get from the dressing room to the stage:

The Half — The time all actors have to be in the building, i.e. thirty-five minutes before curtain up.

The Quarter — Twenty minute warning before the show.

The Five — Ten minute warning.

Beginners — Call to the stage for the actors who appear in the opening scene, five minutes before curtain up.

Many theatrical expressions take the form of directions — off, up, in, out, etc., and these must not be confused:

To **go up** — To begin the performance; also to corpse.

To **come down** — To finish the performance.

To **walk on** – To play a part with no lines.

18

The **walk down** – Parade of grinning actors in ascending order of importance at the end of a show, culminating in the curtain. (Usually only in pantomimes and musicals.)

The **get in** (also known as the **fit-up**) – Time allocated to putting up the set. The opposite of which is not the get out, but the **strike**.

To **go in** – To start a West End run.

To **come in** – As above.

To **enter** – Not as above, but to make your appearance on the stage.

To **get it up** – Not an Onanistic practice, but getting your performance together alone.

To **be off** – To fail to arrive on stage on your cue.

To be **off the book** – To have learned your lines.

To be **on the book** (usually in the form 'not *still* on the book') – Not to have learned your lines.

Now for a few tricks of the trade:

Under-dressing – Method of putting street clothes underneath your costume, usually for the curtain, in order to make a quick get-away to the pub. Also wearing one costume on top of another for a quick change.

Upstaging – Method of taking a step upstage (stage floors usually slope down towards the audience) so that the actor to whom the offending actor is talking has to play his line with his back to the audience.

Rhubarb – What the public believe actors to be repeating when huddled in groups for crowd scenes. In fact only someone trying to be witty might utter this word just to show that he would never dream of using it. The odd Method actor will turn up in a crowd scene in character saying "Ods bodkins, Mercutio, regard the disarray of yon Romeo's viridian hosiery"; most actors are mumbling 'Stewart's tights are falling down', or other topical remarks.

Last Matinée pranks – During the last matinée the actors may play little jokes on each other with the intention of corpsing everyone else. All too often the joker him/her self finds the joke more hilarious than the others do. These include filling the bottles of coloured water and cold tea with real alcohol, dropping plastic dogdirts around the set, swapping costumes with another character, coming on in plastic tartan rainhats, changing lines, e.g. instead of "Would you like a cup of tea?"; "Would you like some haddock mousse?", etc.

Hidden scripts – Quite often an actor finds himself on opening night with the lines not quite learnt. These occasions lead to desperate measures. Pages of script are hastily sellotaped to the back of pieces of furniture and props, lines are written in biro on the cuffs and the back of the hand, and extras can be spotted holding open scripts on their trays or behind their shields, ready to feed lines when necessary.

Now for some frequently used expressions relating to other actors:

See you on the green – See you on stage, often said in lieu of good luck.

O.T.T. – Over the top, said when an actor gives his part more energy than is entirely necessary. Since the expression has been taken up by other sectors of the community, actors mime it instead by pulling a face and at the same time with the right hand (palm downwards) making a horizontal sawing motion about six inches above their heads.

N.A.R. — No acting required, initials seen scribbled in the margin of a leading actor's script next to lines which did not demand any particular degree of virtuosity.

Brave — Description given (in reverent tones) of a performance which the speaker found indescribably embarrassing.

Good value — Said of an actor whose performance, although of the most pitiful quality, is extremely noticeable.

He/she phoned his/her performance in — Said when an actor has apparently sleep-walked through the play.

He/she couldn't act his/her way out of a paper bag — Said of an actor who falls below a certain level of excellence.

He/she couldn't direct traffic — Said of a director who similarly falls below certain standards.

He/she couldn't direct pee into a bucket — As above.

Chorine — Chorus girl.

Actrine — Lesser actress.

Some of the lower orders of the acting profession have invented a whole new use of these theatrical expressions and refer to every experience of life as though it was a performance. This is quite possibly because otherwise they'd have so little opportunity to use the expressions at all.

The cult of Life-As-A-Performance is often demonstrated by adding the word **acting** to any phrase depicting a situation **outside** the theatre, for instance: standing at a bus-stop acting, or doing a lot of biting my nails acting, or quietly trying to get on with eating my dinner acting. The effect is nauseatingly cloying and coy, but the relentless use of this figure of speech is hailed in some circles as wit.

It is just as well for the playgoer to have a handful of stock phrases which can be used after any performance and which will get them out of having to express their opinion at all. This may seem an unnecessary move, but experience will show you that your real opinions will be pooh-poohed by anyone you are foolish enough to express them to. Far wiser to mutter quietly "Have they never HEARD of Brecht?", or "One sometimes longs for the return of Sir Johnston Forbes-Robertson". Useful also to lob the ball squarely into the other court, not by asking what everyone else thinks, which can only expose you as a vacillating fool, but by saying in outraged tones "What ABOUT the second act!" Needless to say

22

great care should be taken in any remark made to the actors. Two fairly safe comments are: "Isn't Ibsen (or whoever) a WONDERFUL playwright" and "The director should be shot."

DO NOT disgrace yourself by using expressions which are only used by amateurs and ill-informed members of the public at large.

DO NOT ask how the actor learns all those lines, or wonder however they came up with that extraordinary make-up, or, even worse, refer to greasepaint.

NEVER describe an out of work actor as 'resting', with or without a knowing look, or describe the profession of acting as 'treading the boards'.

DO NOT suggest that an actor who appears in straight plays is 'legit'. The only actors who are not legit are the ones who never knew their fathers.

DO NOT, whether you mean it or not, wish an actor good luck, but instead shriek jovially "Break a leg!"

And whatever you do, don't go blundering into the famous theatrical **superstitions**, unless you want to find yourself being made to leave the room, turn three times in an anti-clockwise direction, spit, swear and finally beg re-admission before being forgiven. Even if you are forgiven, you are unlikely to be asked back. Never quote from *Macbeth*, which is always referred to as 'The Scottish Play', or by the more daring as 'Maccers'. It is difficult to know where to draw the line on quoting from this particular play. One might get away with saying "God save the King" or "Knock, knock, who's there?", but would stand no chance whatsoever with "Double double, toil and trouble" or "Out damned spot". Macbeth has gained its unlucky reputation because most productions of it seem to be failures. This in turn is often blamed on the Bard himself who is said to have used real black magic incantations for the witches' scenes.

A superstition which is based on a more practical consideration is whistling, or rather, not. In the days before mechanisation the fly-men (frequently ex-sailors and used to dealing with rigging) took their cues to drop scenery and weights from a complex system of whistles. So if you whistled in those days the consequences could have been even worse than the above-mentioned spitting ritual.

Another superstition, which, luckily, only applies to actors, is that they should never leave their soap in the dressing room or they will not work in that theatre again. A pretty good insurance policy in some cases, if only it were true. The fact behind the superstition is probably no more than the hastily fabricated self-justification of some penny-pinching Scrooge trying to explain the mysterious removal of an inch-long piece of scented slime from the wash basin during the final performance.

The breezy manner should be affected by the bluffer at all times. Performers should not be talked about with the reverential use of their whole names. For instance never say "Wasn't Timothy West marvellous!", rather "Timmy was good, wasn't he!" Abbreviated christian names are the order of the day, but tread carefully for some are not standard, e.g:

      Felicity — Foo — Kendal
      Rosalie — Bun — Crutchley
      Dinah — Mousse — Sheridan
      Elizabeth — Paddy — Larner
      Evelyn — Boo — Laye
      Michael — Bodger — Bogdanov
      Robert — Tim — Hardy

In all such special cases use of the surname is essential. And just as one should always refer to Dame Peg (the late Peggy Ashcroft) or Sir John (the one-and-only Gielgud) one would never refer to the unrivalled comedy actress as anything other than "Lovely-Judi-Dench".

The actor-playwright-composer **Ivor Novello** re-titled his shows so that, *Perchance to Dream* became Perchance to Scream, *Careless Rapture,* Careless Rupture and *The Dancing Years,* The Prancing Queers. In this delightful manner of self-mockery, the actress and novelist Dulcie Gray is renamed Gracie Dull.

When you are still in the dressing room it might be suggested that you all "go for a bite at J's" (or "J.A.'s"). This is an invitation for supper at a theatrical restaurant famous for its late hours and its habit of giving your table (which you booked over three months ago) to a minor television star and his lover who have just popped in on the off-chance. Actors continue going there in order to practise **rubber-necking** (scanning other tables to see if there is any-one useful like a casting director to chat up) and **table-hopping** (deserting the friends you came with so you can sit with people who are more interesting, more famous or more useful). Other locations for these activities include The Ivy and Orso's.

Any would-be theatrical bluffer must have at least a sprinkling of facts from theatrical and dramatic history – so here it is.

A POTTED HISTORY

The Greeks Had a Word For It

Theatre, drama, critic, comedian, scene, chorus, dialogue, tyrant, Method, character, crisis, chaos, catastrophe — the most important words in the modern theatrical vocabulary come from ancient Greece.

The theatrical tradition evolved from the ancient **rites** of fertility and of Dionysus, the god of wine, rites which are still actively practised by actors in the British regional repertory theatres.

Productions were paid for by a **Choregus**, a wealthy citizen who was obliged to support the drama as part of his civic duty.

Theatres were built on hillsides and consisted of an **auditorium**, where the audience sat, **scena**, which made up the scenery and an **orchestra** where the actors stood. (The musicians had to sit on steps at the side of the stage.) The actors wore chitons (long shirts), masks, cothurni (high boots rather like the 'wedgies' so fashionable in the early 1970's) and onkos (tall hats). Thus bedecked, looking like absolute burks, they performed classical comedies and tragedies.

The word **comedy** derives from *comos*, meaning revel or masquerade, and, with devastating Greek logic, the word **tragedy** comes from *tragos*, meaning goat.

No women were allowed to appear on stage, and in comedy, to make sure that the audience were left in no doubt which actors were meant to be women, the ones who weren't wore a **phallus**, an imitation penis of a size which would make Tyrone Power sit up and take notice.

The most famous Greek actor was **Thespis** who toured the provinces on the back of a cart. The expression 'on the wagon' may have adequately described Thespis, but can seldom be applied to his descendants, who, however, think it unendingly hilarious to refer to themselves as Thespians. (Presumably because it is the only word in the English language which almost rhymes with Lesbians.) As a playwright Thespis was the prize-winner in the Dionysian festival of 535 B.C.

The father of tragedy, **Aeschylus** (525-456 B.C.), was a soldier who fought at the battle of Marathon. He was responsible for the invention of **dialogue**, as his plays were the first to introduce two actors onstage at the same time, talking to each other. God only knows what plays were like before this brilliant innovation. He wrote 80-90 plays, but only seven of these have survived intact.

The fate of characters in Greek tragedies seem somewhat less outrageous when the deaths of their creators are investigated. Aeschylus himself died in Syracuse when an eagle, mistaking his bald head for a rock, dropped a tortoise on it.

Sophocles (496-406 B.C.) however, managed to live until he was 90, and of his 120 plays 18 won prizes, but only seven are extant. His plays have had much influence on later ages. Freud's complexes are named after Sophocles' characters and Shelley had a volume of his plays in his pocket when he drowned.

Euripides (484-406 B.C.), a recluse, managed to score a survival rate of 18 out of 92 plays, but only won 5 prizes. In the tradition of Aeschylus his end fitted his work for in 408 B.C. he went to stay at the

Court of King Archelaus, whose dogs accidentally tore him to pieces.

So much for tragedy. The two principal comic writers were **Aristophanes** (448-380 B.C.) who wrote bawdy, topical and sophisticated plays designated 'old comedy', while the 'new comedy' was provided by **Menander** (342-292 B.C.), who coined the phrase 'Whom the gods love die young'. Menander was a nephew of **Alexis**. (Another comic poet, no relation to Joan Collins.)

One last innovation of the ancient Greeks was **Aristotelean Theory**. Tutor to Alexander the Great, **Aristotle** came up with the startling thought that a play is an *imitation* of an action, and not the action itself, a theory disregarded by many modern actors and directors. He decided that the point of tragedy was to provoke pity and terror in the spectator. Today the manners of box-office managers have much the same effect.

When in Rome

Latin, the language of Ancient Rome, provides us with more important theatrical words: director, rehearsal, stage, conflict, actor, applause and disaster.

The Romans flew in the face of Aristotelean theory. They didn't want an imitation, they wanted the real thing. For the opening performance of the first permanent theatre, built by Pompey to seat 40,000 spectators, 500 lions and 200 elephants were killed. There were sea battles, water ballets, gladiatorial competitions, chariot races, prostitutes were hired so that the portrayal of sex would be more realistic, and the general tone slipped to that of contemporary televison game shows. In this spirit the audiences were showered not only with perfumed water, but with vouchers for money, groceries, holidays and ultimately, modern apartments.

It was not surprising therefore that although **Seneca** (4 B.C.-65 A.D.) wrote at least a dozen plays, they were only read in private and were not performed in the theatres. Seneca was on nodding terms with all the leading characters from *I Claudius:* Caligula tried to kill him; Messalina accused him of an intrigue with Julia and banished him to Corsica, and he eventually became tutor to Nero, who ordered him to commit suicide, which he did.

A great patron of the theatre, **Nero** was himself something of a playwright and actor. He would regularly star in all-day entertainments in theatres the size of the Roman Coliseum. The citizens of Rome were ordered to attend and no one was allowed to leave during the performances however pressing the reason. We read of women in the audience giving birth, and of men growing so bored that they furtively dropped down over a hundred feet from the back wall. Some even shammed death and were carried away for burial.

Like most patrons of the arts Nero had a healthy respect for actors. He had the leading actor **Paris** executed because he acted better than he did.

The two leading actors of ancient Rome were **Roscius** (died 62 B.C.) and his contemporary **Aesopus**.

Comedy flourished in ancient Rome and produced a number of stock characters: a soldier braggart, a miser, a parasite, identical twins, a resourceful slave, and Frankie Howerd. Roman theatre produced two major comic playwrights:

1. **Terence** (c. 185-159 B.C.), an African-born slave freed in Rome, who wrote urbane comedies which were only appreciated by the elite. He was supposedly lost at sea.
2. **Plautus** (254-184 B.C.), a stage carpenter, who wrote plays which were essentially the first musical comedies, as two thirds of the dialogue was sung.

The Dark Ages

(Not to be confused with the spate of empty theatres in Shaftesbury Avenue a few years ago.) The theatre, like history, vanished at the fall of Rome and did not re-appear until the Middle Ages. St. Augustine, once a fanatical theatre-goer, forbade good Christians to attend the theatre in case they might enjoy it as much as he had done. As a result actors took to wagons again, and like modern buskers, only the really bad ones had the gall to continue.

Middle Age Spread

Into the Middle Ages ragged troupes continued to tour their jugglers, wrestlers, acrobats, dancers, mimics, animal trainers, ballad singers and raconteurs, until each Saturday afternoon at the market place was more like Sunday Night at the London Palladium.

Then the Church stepped in with a neat U-turn. A nun from Gandersheim with the unlikely name of **Hrotswitha** adapted the plays of Terence and became the leading playwright of the middle ages, as well as the first woman playwright.

Then the English church, with the help of the **Town Guilds**, took bible stories and made them into play **Cycles** which are popularly known as **Mysteries** and **Miracles**. It is a mystery why anyone wanted to see them in the first place and a miracle that they were successfully revived by the National Theatre in the 1980's.

Meanwhile over in Italy more actors on wagons were inventing **Commedia Dell'Arte**, unbearably loud and raucous improvised plays with nauseating characters like Harlequin, Columbine, Pierrot and Punch who rushed around hitting everybody with a two-pronged stick known as a **slapstick**. A few actors today claim to be experts in Commedia Dell' Arte. Have no doubt about it, these are desperate men.

The Age of Shakespeare

In 1572 a Parliamentary Ordinance declared that actors were henceforth to be classified as **rogues and vagabonds**, and at last the English tradition of great acting was legally acknowledged.

Four years later **James Burbage** built the first permanent theatre in London. He gave it the astonishing name of The Theatre. His example was followed shortly by the builders of The Curtain, The Swan, The Rose and finally The Globe, which was built by his sons, **Richard** (the first great English actor) and **Cuthbert** (who was Richard's manager, and therefore possibly the first **Agent**), from the timber of the original Theatre.

Christopher Marlowe was the first English playwright to bring plays up to the level of great literature. The atheist son of a shoemaker, Marlowe made a mistake frequently made by modern playwrights: while drinking in a pub in Deptford, he queried the bill and was stabbed to death.

Of the life of **William Shakespeare** we have about five facts. These include the fact that he was born and the fact that he died. This has not prevented him from becoming the most written about person in history. The theatrical potential of Shakespeare's work inspired Adolf Hitler to make the pertinent observation that in no country in the world is Shakespeare so badly played as in England.

Shakespeare's friend and contemporary **Ben Jonson**, influenced by the Roman commentator, **Horace**, insisted on a five act structure, which was taken up by all his contemporaries. He wrote some sprightly **Comedies of Humour**. The Humours bore no relation to anything which might make a person laugh but were part of a medical system in which fluids were thought to govern human nature: the sanguine man was governed by blood, the choleric by bile, the melancholic by black bile and the phlegmatic by a substance readily available on London pavements. Jonson was accorded the honour of being buried in Westminster Abbey. However, in order not to take up too much space, he was buried standing up. (Recent excavations at Westminster Abbey show that the gravediggers made a small mistake, and in fact Ben Jonson was buried upside down.)

Jacobean playwrights wrote in combinations. Take two or three names from the following list, shuffle them at random, and if the result sounds like a local estate agent, you can be sure that a play was the outcome: **Beaumont & Fletcher & Massinger & Heywood & Chapman & Shirley & Dekker & Heywood & Marston & Middleton & Rowley &**

Heywood & Tourneur & Ford. The most famous duo, Beaumont and Fletcher, wrote regularly in tandem until Beaumont did the dirty on Fletcher and got married to someone else. Fletcher then teamed up with Massinger, and the relationship became so close that they were eventually buried in the same grave.

On the accession of James I in 1603, the playwrights kowtowing to the taste of their new monarch (a man who, incidentally, couldn't fit his tongue in his mouth), larded their plays with ghosts, witches, magic and masques (e.g. *Macbeth*). These elements are prominent in the works of the Jacobeans, led by **John Webster** of whom practically nothing is known.

Commonwealth Capers

Thus British theatre flourished until the rise of the **Puritans**. Realising that certain things were enjoyed by the people of Britain, the Puritans banned them. These things included maypoles, hotcross buns, dancing, mince pies, horseracing, Christmas day and the theatre. They also banned the Archbishop of Canterbury; an idea perhaps worth reviewing today.

Meanwhile, of course, theatre in Europe flourished, although it must be said that to the British theatre-goer knowledge of anything foreign need only be slight. Spain produced **Lope de Vega**, a contemporary of Shakespeare, who wrote 2000 plays (including *Fuente*, see page 6); **Cervantes**, who is more famous for the creation of *Don Quixote*, and **Calderon**. France provided the two neo-classical playwrights, **Racine** and **Corneille** and the great comic playwright and actor **Molière** - though many now believe that Molière's best plays were in fact written by the disgraced Corneille.

Restoration Romps

In 1660 the British public, sick of eighteen years quiet family life, welcomed Charles II, the dashing son of the beheaded Charles I, back to rule. Charles had enjoyed his stay in France with its glittering theatrical tradition, so shortly after his accession to the throne he re-established theatre in London, and with his brother James, provided financial as well as moral support.

The new theatres were indoors, and more like today's Shaftesbury Avenue buildings, but much smaller. The actors acted on an **apron** stage, and the **proscenium** arch was where it was meant to be — in front of the scenery. Brilliant trick perspective sets were sometimes embellished by using dwarves and children in grown-ups' clothes behind the proscenium to establish depth.

The King's most welcome innovation was the introduction of the **actress**. Until then all female roles had been played by boys. The most famous of the first generation of actresses, **Nell Gwyn** eventually retired to become his mistress.

The first Poet Laureate, **John Dryden**, wrote far too much, most of it too clever by half. His forte was **heroic** tragedy: bombastic plays in rhyme. He was imitated by **Nathaniel Lee** who, not surprisingly, went mad, and **John Dennis**, who stood up in the middle of a rival production's storm sound effects and gave us the phrase "They've stolen my thunder."

Comedy of Manners was the order of the day and was provided by **William Wycherley**, who went under the nickname 'Manly', the diplomat **Sir George Etherege**, **George Farquhar**, an Irish actor, who fought in the battle of the Boyne before stabbing someone on stage and retiring to a career as a writer (he died broke, while London rocked with the success of his last play *The Beaux Stratagem*), and **John Vanbrugh**, better known as the set-designer for Granada TV's 'Brideshead Revisited'.

The master of the form was **William Congreve**, who is responsible for the quotes 'Hell has no fury like a woman scorned', and 'Music has charms to sooth a savage breast.' He retired from playwriting in 1700, and died in 1729 as a result of a coach accident. He left most of his money to the second Duchess of Marlborough, who used it to build a lifesize working dummy of him which sat with her at table, and is said to have been able to drink, speak and laugh at her jokes. Scandalmongers insisted it also performed a more intimate service.

The first English professional woman writer made her debut in the person of **Aphra Behn**, who earlier had been a spy in the Dutch wars. Apart from writing plays, novels, translations and poems, she also introduced **Thomas Otway** to the theatre by getting him a part in one of her plays. During his first performance, he took one look at the audience and decided to be a playwright. He started the vogue for **Domestic** tragedy, and was himself a bit of one. Not having eaten for some days, a friend is said to have bought him a sandwich, which he ate so greedily that he choked to death.

Shakespeare was given an airing, but was thought too barbarous, so Macbeth's witches sang Italian opera, new characters joined the cast of *The Tempest*, Romeo and Juliet lived happily ever after, as did King Lear and Cordelia, who married Edgar, and Richard III was given a new line which seems to have stuck: 'Off with his head... So much for Buckingham.'

So much for Restoration.

Middle Class Mediocrity

The year 1700 was a turning point in theatrical history. Congreve retired and Dryden died, and the ascendant middle classes started their conversion of the British people into respectable, home-loving, prudes. The theatre was the first thing to suffer.

To the dismay of everyone with even half a wit, **Colley Cibber**, a slimy snob and social climber, became Poet Laureate, and his gutless **Sentimental** comedies led the way. The current tragedy form was true to its name: **Bourgeois**.

The leading comic dramatist of the early century was **Susannah Centlivre**, who, as an actress, specialised in the role of Alexander the Great. Most of her plays, like so many modern comedies, depend on people being stuck in cupboards and behind screens.

The essayists **Steele** and **Addison**, infinitely more successful in their *Tatler* and *Spectator*, provided a few plays, as did **Henry Fielding**. It was during a Fielding production the Prime Minister, incensed by the play, got up on to the stage and punched one of the actors. The next day he initiated the 1737 Licensing Act which introduced censorship to the British theatre in the form of the Lord Chamberlain.

One of the most successful plays of the century which contributed to its enforcement was **John Gay**'s *The Beggar's Opera*. Produced by **John Rich** it was said to have made Gay rich and Rich gay.

Interesting side-effects of the Licensing Act were the lengths to which people were driven to evade it. As only the two Royal theatres in London were licensed to produce straight plays, other ingenious companies were forced to advertise (for instance) a concert during the interval of which was performed, free gratis, the tragedy of *Othello*. Some did productions of plays where

36

every twelfth word was sung, and called them operas; and, as they could not legally charge for tickets to straight plays, some managers charged exorbitant prices for cups of chocolate, and every cup of chocolate purchased entitled the drinker to a free performance of their play.

The term 'legitimate' theatre originated at this time meaning those plays which were approved by the Lord Chamberlain.

Artistically speaking, the mid-century saw reform in the person of actor **David Garrick**, who insisted on a more **naturalistic** approach, and put Stratford-Upon-Avon on the map by holding a Shakespeare festival there. His last words were "Oh dear!"

His contemporary, **Charles Macklin**, had three pauses: the moderate, the long and the grand. When a prompter interrupted his grand pause he rushed offstage, punched him on the nose and returned to enthusiastic applause. He made great improvements in theatrical costume, so that, for instance, Roman senators no longer wore periwigs. It was during an argument over a wig that Macklin fatally stabbed another actor through the eye with a stick. He was found guilty of manslaughter, but his popularity saved him from a prison sentence. It is not surprising that at this time there were attempts to prohibit actors and their children from Christian burial.

Richard Brinsley Sheridan, an MP who chalked up a record five and a half hour long speech in the House of Commons, became sole owner of the Drury Lane theatre at the ridiculous age of 27. He had no problem getting his plays accepted by his own theatre, thank goodness, for in them he managed successfully to marry comedy of manners and sentimental comedy, and put the standard of

British play-writing back on a high level.

For some reason many people think Sheridan wrote Restoration comedies. This is much the same as believing that Harold Pinter writes Victorian melodramas. In the House of commons one day Edmund Burke tried to stage a dramatic moment by throwing a dagger on to the floor of the House and crying "Such is the weapon which French Jacobins would plunge into the heart of our beloved King!" Sheridan took the wind out of his sails with the retort "The gentleman, I see, has brought his knife with him, but where is his fork?"

The night his theatre burnt to the ground he sat drinking next door in the Piazza Coffee House in Covent Garden and when asked what he was doing replied "May not a man be allowed to drink a glass of wine at his own fireside?"

Like many a heroine of the day, his last words were "Alas, I am absolutely undone!"

Oliver Goldsmith wrote only two plays, but he had a busy life. He ran away from university, set up as a doctor but attracted no patients, tried to take holy orders but was rejected by the bishop, decided to run away to America but got stuck at Cork, was then given £50 to start a career in law but lost it at the gambling tables, set out to make the Grand Tour but returned so impecunious that he had to pawn his clothes, and eventually became proof-reader to the novelist Samuel Richardson.

He then took to literature himself, writing essays, novels, poems and at last *She Stoops to Conquer*, one of the finest of all British comedies. The success, however, came too late, and he died £2000 in debt.

Wasn't It Romantic?

The winter of 1808/9 saw both major London theatres destroyed by fire. They were rebuilt, but the replacements were a management's dream and an actor and theatre-goer's nightmare: huge tiered monsters with hopeless accoustics and sightlines, and, of course, higher ticket prices. The audiences expressed their indignation with the type of violence now only seen when a penny is put on to the price of a pint of beer, or Crystal Palace play at home to Chelsea.

Acting thrived with the **Kemble** family, led by **John Philip** and his sister, **Sarah Siddons**, and **Edmund Kean**, who started as a stage Cupid. Kean's preparation for tragic roles included eating raw beef for murderers, roast pork for tyrants and, for lovers, boiled mutton.

British tragic playwriting however hit an all-time low when the Romantic poets, **Shelley**, **Coleridge**, **Byron** and **Keats**, decided that poems divided between twelve characters, were plays.

The Romantics in Germany were much more successful. **Johann Wolfgang Goethe**, who was later given a Von between christian and surname, was not just a clever playwright. He became Minister of Finance at the age of 25, had an attempt at refuting Newton's theory of light and made anatomical history with the discovery of the human intermaxillary bone.

His friend **Friedrich Von Schiller**, after studying law at military academy, qualified as a surgeon. His play *The Robbers* caused a storm all over Europe, but predictably the English banned it before it got here. Schiller had gone AWOL to attend the first night, and was arrested and forbidden henceforward to write anything but medical books. So he ran away and became the leading playwright of the **Sturm und Drang** (storm and stress) movement. He wrote *Don Carlos*, a play twice as long as *Hamlet*, and a couple of plays which make mince-meat of history and geography but are definitely great drama.

Although Goethe and Schiller had an overwhelming influence on world drama, it is quite unnecessary for the British theatre-goer to know anything about them but their names.

Victorian Values & Edwardian Excess

As the nineteenth century rolled on, the British poets (Tennyson, Browning and Swinburne) were still at it, and between them had managed to encourage audiences to stay at home in their thousands. Managers tried to counter this highfalutin drama with theatre for the low-brow, so that in 1879 Matthew Arnold felt free to declare that there was no English theatre — meaning that literary standards had become subservient to showmanship and box-office receipts.

Edmund Kean's son **Charles**, understood perfectly the British need for vulgarity and tried to incorporate as much irrelevant spectacle as possible in his productions of classical plays. Later, **Herbert Beerbohm Tree** did *A Midsummer Night's Dream* with real grass and rabbits. (Both Tree and his wife appeared in it and a contemporary critic complained that you couldn't see the wood for the Trees.) The public, however, were quite happy to have aquadramas, horse-races and Ben Hur's chariot race onstage with no accompanying literary text to clutter up the action. Thus, **Melodrama** thrived.

Henry Irving, the first actor to be knighted, excelled in melodrama, and after his rendition of the telling line "The bells! the bells!" peals of approbation rang through the auditorium. It was however, not the most famous line in Victorian melodrama; the much parodied "Dead! ... and never called me mother!" takes that title, and also the biscuit.

And as in every other century there were more moves towards **Naturalism**. **Madame Vestris** had initiated the **Box Set** (three walled rooms with real doors) and **T.W. Robertson's** seemingly laughable **Cup and Saucer** dramas played on them, and were seen to be a real break away from traditional stereotypical caricatures.

Victorian theatre was run by actor-managers. Apart from the Keans, the Trees, Madame Vestris and Irving, there were innumerable lesser talented but equally grand actor managers whose names sound like small towns in Devon.

The end of the century saw the rise and fall of **Oscar Wilde**, master of the brittle epigram. Described by a contemporary as 'a Roman emperor carved out of suet', Wilde was imprisoned for gross indecency with other male persons, and lived the rest of his life in Paris under the name Sebastian Melmoth.

W.S. Gilbert (full name William Schwenck Gilbert — now you know why he stuck to his initials) was also rather a good playwright until Sir Arthur Sullivan persuaded him to become the very model of a modern major lyricist.

While Continental Europe produced a string of great stars like **Rachel, Réjane, Helena Modjeska**, **Eleanora Duse**, **Thomaso Salvini** and **Sarah Bernhardt**, British acting hit the pits with the emergence of **Lillie Langtry**, known to some as the Jersey Lily and to the Princess of Wales as the Jersey cow.

Also in continental Europe playwrights of incalculable influence, such as **Victor Hugo, Alexandre Dumas, Alfred De Musset, Eugene Scribe, Nikolai Gogol, Alexander Ovstrovsky** and **Ivan Turgenev** were scribbling away, unnoticed by the British.

But there was a group of writers who actually did make some impression in England. Between them **Henrik Ibsen, Anton Chekhov** and **August Strindberg** — a collective which could be termed the North Sea Depression — not only brought bored, syphilitic, misogynists onto the English stage, but managed to infiltrate the British repertoire with a force unrivalled by any other foreigners. So much so, that the average English production of an Ibsen play is usually set in a well-appointed house in Cheltenham with a fjord in the garden.

The works of **Henrik Ibsen** are so drenched in the spirit of his native Norway that he had to go and live in Rome, Dresden and Munich to write them.

Anton Chekhov once claimed "medicine is my lawful wife and literature is my mistress." His mistress was actually an actress with the unlikely name of Olga Knipper. His most popular play *The Seagull* was booed off on its first performance in Moscow. Usually associated with the yawning and sighing of the Naturalism Movement, Chekhov denied that his work was naturalistic. "The stage is art," he claimed. "Kamskoy has a picture on which the faces are painted beautifully. What would happen if one cut out the nose of one of the faces and substituted a real one for it? The nose would be realistic but the picture would be ruined."

Chekhov wrote the plays in which characters drone "Everything would be all right if only we could get to Moscow..." until you feel quite willing to pay their train fare, if only they would just GO.

Chekhov's friend, **Konstantin Stanislavski**, the director of the **Moscow Arts Theatre**, started writing books which one of our leading actresses has described as 'handbooks for bad actors'. In these books Stanislavski explains the elements of performance which are understood instinctively by good actors. This is called the **Stanislavski System** (and should not be confused with the American **Method**, which is altogether another thing).

Johan August Strindberg, a horrid little man, was a leading light in every ism going. At different times he led the way in naturalism, realism, mysticism, romanticism and even expressionism. He hated everything to do with the idea of female emancipation, and managed to blame all the ills of the world on women and in particular his three wives.

Another foreigner, **Richard Wagner**, made less impression on world theatre with his *Ring Cycle* than by putting out the **Houselights**, and leaving the audience in the dark, where they have been ever since.

Twentieth Century Blues

Henry Irving's leading lady, **Ellen Terry** had an illegitimate son, the director and designer **Edward Gordon Craig**, who brought us squarely into the twentieth century and anticipated today's directors by publicly confessing that he would rather work with puppets than actors.

In the twenties and thirties British drama had a field-day. **George Bernard Shaw** wrote hundreds of highly articulate dramas; **Noel Coward** tossed off a handful of sparkling comedies and **Terence Rattigan** bumped up British morale with some jolly stiff-upper-lip plays.

There were a great number of dreadful **Historical** plays about everyone from Clive of India to the Brontë sisters by way of Abigail Masham, which may not have done much for world literature or factual biography, but provided wonderful vehicles for the great new British actors like **Laurence Olivier, Ralph Richardson, Sybil Thorndike, Edith Evans, John Gielgud, Michael Redgrave, Flora Robson, Peggy Ashcroft** and **Donald Wolfit**, who has since been eclipsed by his dresser.

The Second World War seriously disrupted the work of **Bertolt Brecht**, who spent the thirties in Germany trying to create **Epic Ensemble** theatre. Adolf Hitler beat him to it, and Brecht fled to America, where his work on **Political** theatre was upstaged by the McCarthy trials, and poor Brecht fled back to Germany, where he founded the **Berliner Ensemble** and died.

In post war Britain, the **Angry** playwrights, disgusted by plays about verbose middle-class bores in drawing rooms, started writing plays about verbose middle-class bores in kitchens. There were also a few plays, usually by **Samuel Beckett**, set on rubbish tips. These are incomprehensible to everyone except those people who would have been able to see the emperor's new clothes.

Most recently plays have become more like

dramatisations of the leader column of *The Guardian*, discussing 'relevant' subjects like Northern Ireland, unemployment, South Africa, rape, and the problems of lesbian vegetarian nightcleaners in Chile.

A reaction against this worthy work has inspired a style of theatre which caters to the lowest common denominator in British taste: shows which demand a lot in the way of pre-publicity, little in the way of script, nothing in the way of plot or acting, and a performing set.

The American Tragedy

The twentieth century saw America contributing to the canon of world drama with the kind of hyper-emotional plays designed to encourage exactly the type of dreadful over-acting that the American cinema was attempting to wipe out. The main offenders were **Eugene O'Neill**, **Lillian Hellman**, **Clifford Odets**, **Tennessee Williams** and **Edward Albee**.

Oriental Expression

Divinely unaffected by everything that was going on anywhere else in the world, the Japanese painted their faces white and invented the all-male **Noh** theatre. The women, feeling left out, counteracted by inventing all-women **Kabuki** theatre. Rather put out by the competition, the men passed a law banning women from appearing anywhere and declared that henceforth Kabuki would also be all-male. Which all goes to show that there's no business like Noh business, like no business we know ...except Kabuki business that is.

THE CRITICS

How to Decipher Reviews

When the dust-jacket of a novel informs you that Miss X is 'the new Jane Austen', you instantly know that her book is full of bitchy remarks, and any novel written 'in the style of Virginia Woolf' obviously has no plot. Similarly, theatre criticism in the national press can be easily understood once the technical terms used by the modern critic are decoded. Here are some of the critical expressions most frequently encountered:

Accessible — So banal that a child of five would find it simplistic.

Alienation Effect — A device which jars the audience into the uncomfortable awareness that they *are* the audience (e.g. the price of their ticket). (N.B. This is sometimes called by its original German name, **Verfremdungseffekt** — not to be confused with vorsprung durch technik.)

Avant Garde — Even the critic couldn't make head nor tail of it.

Black Comedy — Comedies, plots of which have less to do with underpants than undertakers.

Brechtian production — The company could not afford a set.

Camp — Loud, silly and more often than not involving a homosexual element of which the critic thoroughly disapproves and which he daren't openly criticise for fear of seeming anti-gay.

Comedy of Manners — Epigrammatic plays in which nobody ever says what they mean (e.g. for the line: "Would you like a cup of tea?" read "I would like to rip off your clothes and ravish you now, here on the kitchen table.") These plays can often be recognised by the arch tone employed by the actors appearing in them.

Conflict — Nothing to do with the relationship between director and actors, but the seed of the play itself (e.g. Hamlet wishes to kill his uncle but realises that nice boys don't do such things; to do it or not to do it, that is the conflict).

Deconstructionalist – Anything directed by someone who is under 25.

Delivery – What an actor makes of his lines. Dame Edith Evans' marvellous delivery owed a lot to her dictum: if you don't understand the line, say it as though it's improper.

Dénouement – The moment when everything that you have understood of the plot so far is proved wrong.

Deus ex machina – From the Greek 'God out of a machine'. Now means any contrived piece of plot. (Generally occurs during the dénouement.)

Dialectical – Packed with dull discussions and analytical arguments.

Didactic – Barrel-thumping, axe-grinding political preaching of the lowest order.

Ensemble – On-stage camaraderie achieved at the cost of much malicious back-stage backbiting.

Epic production – A production that is still going on long after the pubs have shut.

Exposition – Scenes generally between a housemaid and an elderly spinster aunt setting up the story so far, e.g: Housemaid: "Times is hard now that Master Giles has had to sell the Bentley and take up basket-weaving to pay us servants' meagre wages, and what with Madam being elected chairperson of the Jockey Club, and Miss Prowse now happily married and living in Java, it's fair given me and MacDonald, the new butler, the colly-wobbles." To which the maiden aunt can only reply: "And how is Bill Taylor taking all this this?"

Feminist– Productions in which over five per cent of the company are women.

Grand Guignol– The type of grotesque over-acting practised mainly by actresses wearing ill-fitting wigs with lipstick on their teeth.

High Comedy – Comedy without any laughs.

Method – American bastardisation of the Stanislavski system of acting. The resultant performance usually convinces no-one but the person who is giving it.

Motivation — The driving force behind an actor's line (e.g. behind the line "Would you like a cup of tea?" might be the motivation "I really must get rid of these cash and carry caterers' teabags.")

Naturalism — The depiction of life at its most boring.

Pinteresque — Scanty monosyllabic dialogue with pauses you could drive a train through.

Poetic — Long-winded and over written.

Polemic — The argument of a play. Sometimes goes like this:
X: Would you like a cup of tea?
Y: No.
X: Oh yes you would.
Y: Oh no I wouldn't
X: Oh yes you would.
Y: Oh no I wouldn't ... etc.

Polished — Over-rehearsed and smug.

Political – Sympathetic to the Left.

Post Modernist – Sparse production with simple set and neon lighting.

Realism – The depiction of life at its most tawdry.

Song stylists – Performers who can really sell a **number** (song) but who could not *buy* their way into the chorus at La Scala.

Stylish – Adjective used to describe virtuosity combined with confidence and economy. Now only used when describing men in silk dressing gowns.

Technique – Long forgotten acting art of being heard and finding your light.

Theatre of the Absurd – The theatre's answer to surrealism. In a typical scene a grenadier guard wearing a Bluebell girl's head-gear might hand a boa-constrictor to a charwoman (who is quietly whistling Mendelssohn's Wedding March) with the line "Would you like a cup of tea?"

Theatre of Cruelty – Theatre designed to make the audience suffer. This term can be freely used about most contemporary work.

Tour de Force – Involving a lot of shouting. Not to be confused with **Forced to Tour** a condition experienced by middle-aged television personalities.

Vernacular – Anything said to have been 'written in the vernacular is more likely to have been written in the lavatory – copied down from the stuff scrawled on the back of the door.

Well-made play– Over-structured work, the only fault of which is that it is deadly dull.

Working Class Theatre – Theatre cultivated to instil a sense of well-being and smug superiority in an audience of middle-class pseudo-intellectuals.

FACT AND FICTION

Time to explode a few theatrical myths and exhibit a few fascinating theatrical facts.

1. **Sarah Bernhardt** had a wooden leg ... **False**. (We do not mean that she had a false leg.) At the grand old age of 72, gangrene set in on the leg which had given Sarah Bernhardt trouble all her life. En route to the operating theatre she confidently whistled the Marseillaise. After a slow recovery she was brought a wooden leg. After a few unsuccessful tries at screwing it on she screamed and threw it into the fire. She did not get a replacement, and refused to have a wheelchair. Instead she was carried around in a litter, and called 'Mère La Chaise'. The French custom of three knocks to signal curtain-up inspired wags to cry out "Here she comes!", but even in performance she still refused artificial aids and said "In case of necessity I shall have myself strapped to the scenery." In fact she lay on a couch and at dramatic moments threw herself with superhuman force into the arms of the man playing opposite her. In a typical gesture of American good taste the manager of P.T. Barnum's touring circus, hearing the news of her unfortunate amputation, telegrammed an offer of $10,000 for the offending leg, which he wished to exhibit.

2. The longest running play in the world is by a woman ....**True**. Despite a feeble dénouement in which an intelligent and highly articulate detective turns into a raving lunatic within a matter of seconds, *The Mousetrap* by Agatha Christie is still regularly putting out the 'House

51

Full' notices. The shortest run was probably *The Intimate Revue* of 1930, which didn't even manage to complete the first performance before closing forever.

Many leading playwrights have experienced flops. After the first performance of Noel Coward's *Sirocco* the audience booed for 10 minutes and then the leading lady, Frances Doble, gave a curtain speech saying it was the happiest night of her life. Despite a cast which included Lee Remick and Angela Lansbury, Stephen Sondheim's 1964 musical *Anyone Can Whistle* only ran for eight days; the director of Lionel Bart's *Twang!*, Joan Littlewood, left before the first night of the provincial try-out and the subsequent London run went with a dull thud; and the combined talents of Andrew Lloyd Webber, Alan Ayckbourn and P.G. Wodehouse couldn't save their musical *Jeeves* from critical and public indifference.

Some flops were simply asking for it:the Thomas à Becket musical *Thomas and the King* included a song '*Will no-one rid me?*'; *Two Cities* based on Dickens' Tale of ... had Madame Defarge singing 'The Knitting Song', and the Henry VIII musical *Kings and Clowns* gave Henry a song *Get rid of her!* (Presumably it was reprised five times.)

3. 'Bloody' was the first swear word to be heard on the English stage .... **False**. Before the 1737 Licensing Act no-one knows what people got away with. Certainly many words in Shakespeare are much more dubious than Shaw's use of 'bloody'. During a Restoration production an actress got into a bit of a fluster and omitted the 'o' from the word 'Count' in the line "Oh my dear Count!" which 'put the house into such a laughter that London Bridge at low water was silence to it.'

The Lord Chamberlain eventually legalised the word 'bloody' in Shaw's *Pygmalion* in 1912, but there was such a furore that it was not heard on stage again until Noel Coward's 1936 playlet *Red Peppers*. More interesting than the words allowed by the Lord Chamberlain's office were the words refused. Examples include replacing the words 'shit' with 'it', 'balls' with 'testicles', 'crap' with 'jazz', 'post-coital' with 'late evening', 'piss off, piss off, piss off!' with 'shut your steaming gob!', 'wind from a duck's behind' with 'wind from Mount Zion' and 'the perversions of the rubber' with 'the kreupels and blinges of the rubber' — whatever they may be.

4. Frank Sinatra was the first performer to employ a claque to cheer himself along .... **False**. In Paris in 1820 a Monsieur Sauton set up an agency to provide claqueurs for any artiste or management who felt that it would help their opening night. He could provide 500 or more professional clappers, applauders and general enthusiasts per show, divided into the following types:

— the Rieurs who would laugh at jokes and puns,
— the Pleureurs (mainly women) who would hold their handkerchieves to their eyes at the moving parts,
— the Chatouilleurs employed to keep the audience in good humour,
— the Bisseurs who cried "bis!" or "encore!" at the curtain, and
— the Commissaires who were to commit the piece to memory and be noisy in pointing out the merits of structure, witty lines, etc.

5. 'My Fair Lady' is so called from the words of the nursery rhyme 'London Bridge is falling down, my fair lady' .... **False**. The Dick-Van-Dyke-Cor-Blimey-Mite school of Americanised Cockney came up with the astonishing notion that this was the way a Londoner might pronounce the name of the London district of Mayfair, and that Eliza Doolittle's ambition was therefore to be a Myfair Lady. (Then why not a Myfair Lydy?) The name has cropped up from time to time on the American musical scene. The 1925 Gershwin musical *Tell me More* started life as *My Fair Lady*, and his 1926 *Oh Kay!* had been *Miss Mayfair*. Lerner and Loewe's *My Fair Lady* itself emerged as *My Lady Liza* and adolesced as *The Talk of London* before becoming the fully fledged *My Fair Lady* in 1956.

6. Nell Gwyn was really a whore who sold oranges .... **False**. Although Eleanor Gwyn came from a very poor background, and spent much of her childhood working in a 'bawdy house', the evidence is that she was not herself a prostitute but only poured drinks for the customers. At thirteen she spent a few weeks selling oranges and at fourteen she started her short but very successful acting career.

The Poet Laureate, Dryden, wrote many challenging roles specifically for her, and she became one of the most popular players for speaking prologues and epilogues, the Restoration equivalent to a spot as a stand-up comic. She left the stage when Lord Buckhurst made her his mistress (with the proviso that she must give up her career), but he dumped her and she went back to work two months later. When King Charles, intoxicated by her wit and stage style, made her his official mistress she retired for good, and was by all accounts a good and faithful lover. She bore him sons who received titles from their father, but she refused all offers of a title for herself. Charles' dying words were "let not poor Nelly starve". She continued to visit the theatre and became patroness of many promising young talents.

7. Shakespeare wrote 37 plays . . . . **False**. No one is quite sure how many plays, if any, were written by the famous 'bard of Avon'. Plays never included in the Collected Works but sometimes attributed to William Shakespeare include *Sir Thomas More, Edward III*, and *The Two Noble Kinsmen* (on which he is supposed to have collaborated with John Fletcher) and a very dull play indeed called *Edmund Ironside*. Published as a 'lost' Shakespeare play, computer analysis immediately proved that it was, in fact, the work of **Richard Green**, his arch rival who referred to Shakespeare as that "upstart crow". Some people doubt that Shakespeare the player wrote any plays. Some think he might have written the poorer stuff and acted as fence for someone unable to present himself as a playwright. The main contenders for authorship of the Shakespeare canon include Sir Francis Bacon (the Lord Chancellor), Christopher Marlowe (the playwright), Edward de Vere, 17th Earl of Oxford (Court wit and scholar), Sir Walter Raleigh (the soldier and traveller who brought us tobacco and potatoes), Michel Angelo Florio (a defrocked monk, tutor to Lady Jane Grey) and Anne Whately (a lame nun).

8. It is **Traditional** for men to play women's roles but not vice versa ....**False**
Until this century **drag** roles for men (because their costumes dragged on the floor) were probably seen less frequently than **breeches** parts for women (obvious reason), and not only at Panto time. Recent times have thrown up all-male As You Like Its, Oresteias, Julius Caesars, Anthony and Cleopatras, male Helens of Troy, Ladies Macbeth and Bracknell and a disastrous cross-cast Troilus and Cressida. The only male role which seems to have maintained its female tradition is Hamlet. In the eighteenth and nineteenth centuries many actresses specialised in Breeches roles. The popularity of this tradition is thought by some to be based on the desire of men to see women's legs. However this theory does not explain away the fact that audiences in general consist of more women than men, or that most all-female castings of plays were done at the request of groups of upper class women.

Among the parts often played by women in the past were Alexander the Great in Lee's *The Rival Queens*, Macheath in Gay's *The Beggar's Opera*, George Barnwell in Lillo's *The London Merchant*, Lord Foppington in Vanbrugh's *The Relapse*, Sir Harry Wildair in Farquhar's *The Constant Couple*, Bayes in Buckingham's *The Rehearsal*, Roderigo in *Othello* and Cardinal Wolsey in *Henry V*, the title roles in De Musset's *Lorenzaccio* and Rostand's *L'Aiglon*. Plays which have received the all-female treatment include Beaumont and Fletcher's *Philaster*, Killigrew's *The Parson's Wedding*, Settle's *Pastor Fido,* Dryden's *Secret Love* and Congreve's *Love For Love.*

9. Abraham Lincoln was assassinated by an actor .... **True**. John Wilkes Booth shot the American President during a performance of *Our American Cousin* at the Ford Theatre in Washington in 1865. Undoubtedly Lincoln would only have lived a few months more even if he had not been shot, because he was suffering from a still incurable congenital disease. "But-apart-from-that,-what-did-you-think-of-the-play,-Mrs-Lincoln?"-jokes have kept the story in popular imagination. Actors' good deeds are not so well remembered. In London alone three institutions owe their very being to the generosity of actors: Burbage's chief rival, Edward Alleyn, the star of Marlowe's tragedies, founded and endowed Dulwich College; the annual boat race from London Bridge to Chelsea was started, and prize awarded by the Restoration actor Thomas Dogget, who also gave it his name — Dogget's Coat and Badge; and apocryphal evidence points to Nell Gwyn being the founder of Chelsea Hospital, home of the Chelsea Pensioners and the annual flower show.

10. Big Ben is a clock .... **False**. Big Ben is actually the bell housed behind the clock in the Victorian Houses of Parliament. Before 1856 when it was over-shadowed by this national monument, the expression Big Ben was a theatrical term meaning a good or bumping benefit performance. The profits from such a performance went to the specific actor on whose behalf the benefit was held. And so a Big Ben provided actors with a nice supplement to their weekly wage.

QUOTABLE QUOTES

Here are some quotes which it might be worth learning so that you can toss them out with carefree aplomb whenever the situation might present itself. They will be equally at home as interval chit-chat and as conversation fillers when dining out with professionals.

'The only way to see the value of a play is to see it acted.'
Voltaire

'Visiting the theatre leads to fornication, intemperance, and every kind of impurity.'   St. John Chrysostom

'This writing of plays is a great matter.'   G.B. Shaw

'How hard a thing 'twould be to please you all.'
Congreve

'Plays and playhouses came originally from the devil himself.'   William Prynne

(describing what his own plays are about)
'The weasel under the cocktail cabinet.'   Harold Pinter

(on *A Midsummer Night's Dream*)
'The most insipid ridiculous play that ever I saw in my life.'   Samuel Pepys

(on theatrical entertainment)
'Gay, trifling and directly opposite to the spirit of industry and close application to business.'   John Wesley

'I divide all productions into two categories: those I like and those I don't like.'   Anton Chekhov

'People don't do such things!'   Henrik Ibsen

CHOOSING WHAT TO SEE

Of course any would-be theatrical bluffers must put themselves through the chore of occasionally going to the theatre. Reading books about this subject can never be enough. On opening your daily paper at the entertainment column you will be bombarded by hundreds of plays that will 'run and run', musicals which will make you want to 'jump up and sing', comedies that will have you 'rolling in the aisles' and thrillers which will have you on the 'edge of your seat', which is all a bit disturbing when you also take into consideration how much that seat is going to cost you. So here are a few rules that can help you make sure your money is well spent:

1. Don't bother with **Smash Hits**. You will see so many excerpts on television and read so many interviews with the director, actors, designer, producer, writer, backers and usherettes that you will not only know the plot and most of the dialogue, but also the colour of the leading lady's knickers and where the choreographer goes on holiday. And more's the pity, so will everyone else who speaks English and lives this side of the equator. As a result, any contribution you can make to discussions on the subject of this production can undoubtedly be topped by someone who REALLY knows what's going on.

2. If you insist on visiting a **Classic**, and are thinking of bringing up the subject in public do make sure you read at least a synopsis of the play before you get there. This will give you a sound basis should you wish to comment on the idiocy of cutting such and such a character and the inspired novelty of

setting Hamlet, Prince of Denmark, in contemporary Los Angeles. It will also give you the confidence to dismiss (with raised eyebrows and a sneer) the designer's coup of dressing all the characters in dungarees and Noddy hats.

3. Get your skates on and rush to anything which 'must close Saturday', particularly if it only opened last Monday. The main advantage of witnessing short-run **Flops** is that you're bound to be one of only a couple of hundred who do — and most of those will be the family of the cast. These delightful gems of theatre-going will give you miles of dinner-table chit-chat, and quite possibly a good laugh into the bargain.

4. See every visiting **Foreign Company** (particularly the lesser known ones), for most of the reasons cited in rule 3 above. Only replace the last sentence: it will give you miles of dinner-table chit-chat and quite possibly a wonderful night out into the bargain.

5. Avoid **Previews**, except as novelty viewing. As most directors do (quite rightly) use them as public try-outs, you could easily find yourself discussing the ludicrous use of live pigeons in the opening scene, or the absurd curtain line to act two, only to find that they had been cut before the first night. You will thereby expose yourself as a cheapskate (preview tickets are slightly cheaper) and a bit of a vulture (most professionals would prefer their work to be judged only after the official first night).

6. **First Nights** are always worth a try. Better to get

in first if it's a hit, and if it's dreadful there are usually lots of interesting people in the audience to gawp at when the going gets tough.

7. Look out for actors who don't seem to have been hailed by the critics and follow their career. Acting as **Talent Scout** is always fun, and if you're bright enough you could spot someone who does actually become SOMEONE. This will give you a valuable line in "Didn't I always say they were marvellous?" conversations, which can be filled out with "I'll never forget her rendition of French maid in *The Whore ... the Merrier!* at Skegness Rep before it became an ice rink."

THE AUTHOR

The repertoire of world drama as experienced by the author:

Ancient Greece: The Chorus of Euripides' 'The Phoenician Women'.

Ancient Rome: Nothing. (Well, everyone says they're not meant to be performed.)

Miracles and Mysteries: Mercifully, avoided so far.

Age of Shakespeare: Played Hippolyta in Fletcher and Massinger's 'The Custom of the Country', Isabella in Webster's 'The White Devil' and Putana in Ford's 'Tis Pity She's a Whore'.

Restoration: Author of *The Female Wits*; played Mrs Marwood in Congreve's 'The Way of the World'.

Early 18th century: Directed Mrs Centlivre's 'Wedlock/Deadlock' and 'The Basset Table', and Pergolesi's 'La Serva Pardonna; co-adaptor with Giles Havergal of Samuel Richardson's *Pamela;* played Brigida in Goldoni's 'Country Life' and Lucrezia in his 'The Impresario From Smyrna'.

Romantic Drama: Played Queen Elizabeth in Schiller's 'Mary Stuart'.

Victorian and Edwardian: The Duchess of Berwick in Wilde's Lady Windemere's Fan, Metalla in Offenbach's 'La Vie Parisienne' (in a translation entitled 'French Knickers'), Polina in Chekhov's 'The Seagull' and Clara Hibbert in 'The Vortex'.

20th century: Ruth in Coward's 'Blithe Spirit', Kadija in Genet's 'The Screens', the Mother in Brecht's 'The Mother', Mrs Peachum in his 'Threepenny Opera', various suffering Germans in his 'Fears and Miseries of the Third Reich, the title role in 'Arturo Ui', Augustias in Lorca's 'House of Bernarda Alba' and Crawshaw in Christopher Hampton's 'Savages'.

Oriental Theatre: The author is a woman.

THE BLUFFER'S GUIDES®

Available at £1.99 and (new titles* £2.50) each:

Accountancy
Advertising
Antiques
Archaeology
Astrology & Fortune Telling
Ballet
Bird Watching
Bluffing
British Class
Chess
Champagne*
The Classics
Computers
Consultancy
Cricket
Doctoring
The European Community
Finance
The Flight Deck
Golf
The Green Bluffer's Guide
Japan
Jazz
Journalism
Literature
Management
Marketing

Maths
Modern Art
Motoring
Music
The Occult
Opera
Paris
Philosophy
Photography
Poetry
P.R.
Public Speaking
Publishing
Races, The
Rugby
Secretaries
Seduction
Sex
Skiing*
Small Business*
Teaching
Theatre
University
Weather Forecasting
Whisky
Wine
World Affairs

These books are available at your local bookshop or newsagent, or can be ordered direct. Prices and availability are subject to change without notice. Just tick the titles you require and send a cheque or postal order for the value of the book, and add for postage & packing:

UK including BFPO — £1.00 per order
OVERSEAS including EIRE — £2.00 per order

Ravette Book Orders, P O Box 11, Falmouth, Cornwall TR10 9EN.